STEP-BY-STEP GARDEN PROJECTS

Peter McHoy

Brickwork

How to build paths, patios, walls,
pillars, steps, ponds and barbecues

AURA

Step-by-Step Garden Projects Brickwork

Peter McHoy

Copyright © 1999
Aura Books plc

Produced by Transedition
Limited, Oxford OX4 4DJ,
England

Editing and layout: Asgard
Publishing Services, Leeds

Typesetting: Organ Graphic,
Abingdon

Picture credits
All photographs by the author
except as follows: CAMAS 2–3,
33, 43; Marshalls Mono Ltd 23,
25, 37, 62, 79. All drawings by
Colin Fargher, Fargher Design,
Douglas, Isle of Man.

10 9 8 7 6 5 4 3 2 1

Printed in Dubai

ISBN 1 901683 02 8

Peter McHoy has worked on six gardening magazines, three of them as editor, but now devotes most of his time to writing and photography. He has written about 50 books, most of them on gardening, and contributes regular gardening features to *Water Gardener*, *Park Home* and *Practical Householder*. He also runs a horticultural photographic library of his own pictures, and acts as consultant to several publishers.

His approach to gardening has always been down-to-earth and practical, and he enjoys garden improvements of all kinds. In this book he shares his knowledge in an easy-to-follow manner with plenty of step-by-step illustrations to help you on the way to success with your own garden improvements.

CONTENTS

Building blocks

Garden improvements that involve building with bricks or walling blocks are a lot easier than they may sometimes look; and they don't have to be hard work, either. You simply need to take your time with the projects, and use appropriate tools. Whether you're paving a patio, building a garden wall, or making a plinth for a garden ornament, building things can be superbly satisfying; and it's a lot cheaper than getting someone else to do it.

This book sets out with the assumption that you have no significant experience of brick-laying or working with walling blocks, so don't be deterred if you haven't tackled this kind of DIY job before. Within the limitations of space, we've packed in a lot of basic techniques and a wide range of projects for you to try.

It's impossible to deal with all the different bricklaying and construction methods, but if you're tackling simple garden construction jobs, then you're well advised to keep to simple methods anyway. If you'd like a tall, 'crinkle-crankle' (wavy-edged) boundary wall, then it's best to consult a specialist — but most of us are happy with the kinds of project described in this ideas-packed book.

Using the book

To get an idea of the projects that might appeal to you, just glance down the contents list, or flick through the illustrations. And remember that you may well be able to modify one of our projects, or even build something completely different using the same approach.

Once you've mastered the basic principles for one project, it's easy to apply the knowledge to something else. To save space and avoid a lot of repetition, we use cross-references later in the book to take you back to earlier pages where particular techniques are described in detail.

For instance, footings (foundations for walls) are constructed in much the same way whether you're building a boundary wall, a raised bed or a retaining bank. And similarly, bricklaying techniques are much the same whatever you happen to be building.

We've tried to keep jargon to a minimum, but sometimes technical terms are unavoidable, especially when you have to order materials. Where this is the case, you'll find a useful glossary of terms on pages 76-79.

You may need to buy some of your materials from a builders' merchant. This may seem intimidating at first, especially if you're surrounded by specialist tradesmen, but it needn't be. You'll find that most builders' merchants are very helpful, and very generous with their advice, if you simply explain what you need and what it's for.

Picking a project

The projects in the following pages cover two main areas: paving and walls. Paving can be used for paths or patios. And walls aren't just boundary walls — they can just as easily form part of a raised bed. You'll probably find paving projects the easiest to start with, and it's a good idea to get your hand in on a path before you tackle the patio. Once you've mastered laying a small area of paving, you'll be confident with larger areas.

Walls aren't difficult to build, but small errors of alignment or level are much more obvious. Paving can be a little more forgiving! If you've never done any bricklaying before, start with a

Concrete walling blocks and paving slabs may often be a good alternative to bricks. You can buy them in a wide range of sizes, finishes and colours. They're ideal if you want to link raised beds, and perhaps steps, with a patio area. However, you'll need to bear in mind that they are usually heavier to lift and lay than bricks.

quick-and-easy project such as a plinth or a barbecue. Once you've completed one project successfully, you'll be a lot more confident — and that garden wall won't seem quite such a daunting task.

Buying materials

Most of us appreciate that concrete paving slabs and walling blocks come in many forms, each with its own mood message. Bricks, on the other hand, are often taken for granted. It's worth getting better acquainted with the many different types available. Some are more suitable than others for garden use, and they also come in a surprising range of surface textures and colours.

You might find a selection of concrete blocks, pavers and bricks at your local garden centre or at a large DIY store, but the range you'll see there is often very limited. It's well worth sending off for the catalogues of manufacturers who sell garden walling and paving. Some of these will supply direct, which makes a lot of sense. It isn't a good idea to carry heavy building materials like bricks and blocks in the boot of your car.

You may also find a good selection of bricks and blocks at your local builders' merchant. In fact this will probably be your best source of supply for most small garden construction projects. But if you see a brick that you like, be sure to check that it's recommended for paths or garden walls. If in doubt, phone the manufacturer.

Don't dismiss paths as uninteresting projects. This one transforms a sloping lawn and border into a very special garden scene. There's no complicated bonding pattern — just rows of bricks in line — but they've been laid in a magical curve that demonstrates a strong sense of design.

What you may need

You may already have some of the everyday tools that are needed for garden DIY jobs such as laying paving or bricks. Even so, most of the tools described here are well worth buying specifically for the jobs described in this book. You're sure to find additional uses for many of them. For instance, if you don't already have a plumb-bob, it will come in extremely handy for

These are some of the tools it's well worth buying if you don't already have them (roughly from left to right): **1** *spirit-level;* **2** *bricklayer's trowel;* **3** *pointing trowel;* **4** *raking tool;* **5** *line and pins;* **6** *measuring tape;* **7** *bolster chisel;* **8** *plumb-bob;* **9** *cold chisel;* **10** *club hammer;* **11** *rubber mallet;* **12** *line blocks and pins;* **13** *float trowel.*

paper-hanging. And a club hammer and mallet have many uses around the home and garden.

Some tools (such as a builder's square) can be improvised or made from scrap wood. You don't need to buy expensive equipment like a block splitter or a flat-plate vibrator. You'll only use them once or twice, so you can hire them instead.

Tools to buy
Absolutely essential tools include a spirit-level (the longer the better), bricklaying and pointing trowels, a club hammer and a bolster chisel. An ordinary cold chisel is also useful, while a wooden or rubber mallet is less likely to

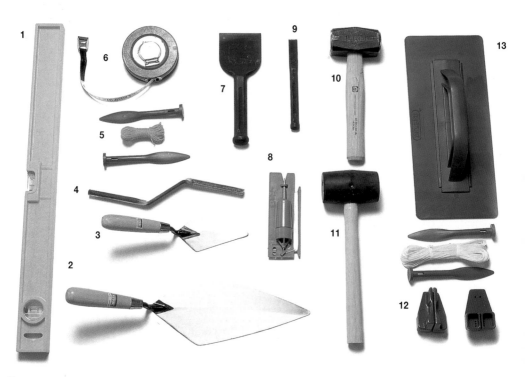

damage the brick or block than a club hammer if you have to use the head.

A long measuring tape will be invaluable when it comes to marking out the area. Don't consider anything shorter than about 30 ft (10 m). You can always use string for marking out an area and to ensure you keep to straight lines — but lines and pins are cheap, and they're rather more suitable for garden use.

For brick or block walls you'll also need lines and pins to ensure that you keep the courses straight! Some of these also include corner blocks to help you stretch the line between the corners of a brick wall.

If you do a lot of bricklaying or paving, it's worth buying a raking tool. You can use a pointing trowel (or improvise) to create neat mortar joints, but a raking tool will speed up the job and ensure a smart finish.

There are some essential tools that you can make yourself, some of which are illustrated below.

Tools to make

A straight-edge is essential. You use it to ensure that paving is laid to an appropriate level or fall — and all you need is a piece of wood about 8-10 ft (2.5-3 m) long. Make sure it has straight, parallel sides and is not warped or distorted.

You can also make a levelling board from a length of spare timber. This needn't be shaped for most purposes, but you may have to cut notches in the ends to the thickness of the paving if you're preparing a sand bed for clay or concrete pavers or blocks.

A builder's square is useful for establishing right angles. You can easily make one from a few lengths of scrap timber. Just screw together three lengths of timber of an appropriate size. It doesn't matter about the exact size of the square, but the proportions when assembled must be 3:4:5 (see illustration below). The finished square will make a 90° angle.

You can also make pegs and spacers from scrap wood for pavers that require an even gap.

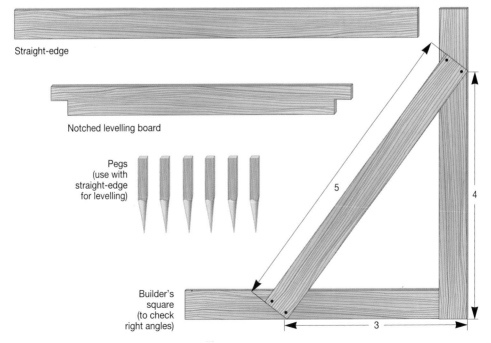

Straight-edge

Notched levelling board

Pegs
(use with
straight-edge
for levelling)

5

4

Builder's
square
(to check
right angles)

3

Tools to hire

Some of the projects in this book call for the use of expensive tools for just a limited period. It's often best to hire these, especially if you're not likely to use them for other jobs in the foreseeable future. Purchasing will make the job expensive, and afterwards you'll have to find somewhere to store what can often be bulky equipment.

Where from?

There are tool-hire companies in most large towns, and they can usually deliver and collect large items. They will almost certainly be able to supply concrete mixers, angle grinders, post-hole borers and flat-plate vibrators.

For how long?

Plan your jobs carefully, so that you know how long you'll need to have the equipment. And don't book it too far ahead. The job may go

Buying second-hand: an alternative to hiring

If you're likely to need a hire tool for a long period, consider buying one second-hand. Look at the classified advertisements in trade and DIY magazines, and in local newspapers. You may be able to buy one for little more than it would cost to hire the tool for a fairly long period.

more slowly than you expect, or the weather could work against you. Most tools are hired by the day or by the week.

You can also minimise hiring costs by making sure that all preliminary work is completed first; and — if applicable — you can arrange to do several jobs that need a particular tool at the same time.

Mixing boards

It's sometimes possible to mix concrete and mortar in small quantities on the ground, close to the point of work. You may want to do this on an old board to prevent contamination with soil.

In an established garden, however, things can be more difficult, especially if you're working in a confined area. It may be hard to stop run-off, or even concrete or mortar, from getting onto flower beds or existing paving.

If you've nowhere convenient to mix up your materials, buy a plastic mixing board (available from large DIY stores). These have a lip to stop run-off from staining paving or contaminating soil, but they still provide enough space for mixing.

Some useful tools that are worth hiring

It's not just large or very expensive tools that are worth hiring. Crowbars, picks and sledge hammers are all cheap to hire, and you may prefer this to buying your own if you're not going to use them very often.

The items listed below are some that you might want to consider, but you may find others useful for a particular job. The larger tool-hire companies provide some very helpful illustrated catalogues.

Angle grinder

This tool is used for cutting bricks and paving slabs neatly. It's noisier and dustier than a block splitter, but good for cutting difficult angles.

Block splitter

A very useful tool for cutting slabs, pavers and bricks to size. It's easy to use, and invaluable if you have a lot of slabs or pavers to cut.

Concrete mixer

Everyone understands what a concrete mixer is for, but you may have to choose between a petrol and an electric version. Petrol-powered mixers are less powerful and smaller, but you will probably find them easier to use, especially for a small job.

Crowbar

Consisting of an iron bar, usually with a beak-like end, this is used for breaking up ground or concrete, and for levering.

Flat-plate vibrator

This machine is used for vibrating sand between clay or concrete pavers, and for consolidating hardcore. You can manage without one, but if you're bedding a lot of paving on sand, it's well worth hiring this tool. It will make a better job of the compaction, and it will make the task easier too.

Pick

The pick, with its long handle and pointed or chisel-ended head, is useful for many construction jobs. It's especially useful for breaking up hard ground.

Sledge hammer

If you have some hardcore to break up or consolidate, this heavy hammer can be invaluable. It's also useful for driving posts or stakes into the ground.

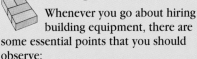

Hiring checklist

Whenever you go about hiring building equipment, there are some essential points that you should observe:

1 Always make sure that you know how to use the tool before accepting it. If you don't know, always be prepared to ask — and if possible obtain written instructions.

2 Use protective clothing and safety spectacles where applicable (good hire shops usually sell these).

3 Check for obvious defects before accepting the tool, and make sure the hire shop is aware of them. Be especially careful to check wiring for signs of wear or loose connections.

4 Don't ever accept anything that looks potentially hazardous. If necessary, try another hire shop.

Cutting bricks

Bricks and coping can be cut in much the same way as paving slabs (see page 22), using a club hammer and bolster chisel. But the result will be much neater, especially for the coping, if you hire an angle grinder to cut them. This is highly recommended if you have to mitre corners, or cut bricks or coping at an angle.

Choosing paving

You should always take time to choose an appropriate paving material. There's such a bewildering variety of slabs and pavers, in a surprising choice of shapes and sizes, not to mention finishes — and then there's the vital question of what colour to choose.

First you need to take into account the size of your garden and the area being paved. For a small area, small units of paving — like bricks or pavers — will probably look better than large paving slabs.

Never be too rigid in your approach. Your paving doesn't have to use just one material, or one kind of slab or paver. Mixing materials can be very effective, and will probably give your garden a stronger sense of design. Don't be afraid to mix clay pavers with concrete paving slabs. Even wood can be used to break up an area of paving that might otherwise look monotonous.

Bricks

We've all admired old brick paths, which blend so naturally with surrounding plants. And a visit to a good builders' merchant will reveal a large range of bricks in some surprisingly warm and interesting colours and textures. But beware: many of them will be perfectly suitable for the wall of a house but completely unsuitable for paving. On the ground, they are attacked by water from all sides, and it will penetrate deep into the brick. When this water freezes, it can cause vulnerable bricks to flake or crumble.

So always check with the supplier that the bricks you're buying are suitable for paving.

Clay pavers

From a distance these resemble bricks, though there are shaped and interlocking kinds as well as the rectangular form. But they're usually thinner than bricks, and the surface dimensions allow them to be laid without mortar joints. Because they're made specifically for paving, you can also be confident that they won't crumble or flake.

Concrete blocks and setts

There are also concrete versions of the clay paver, and they can look more appealing than they sound, especially for a drive.

Small rectangular or shaped blocks are sometimes called 'setts', and the wedge-shaped ones are ideal for forming curves and circles. These can be used to create all kinds of intricate patterns.

Paving slabs

Concrete slabs are still one of the most popular choices for gardens, perhaps because they are quick and easy to lay. They don't have to look boring: there are many different finishes, some of which bear a convincing resemblance to natural stone.

You can create more interesting patterns by mixing slabs of different sizes. In fact, most manufacturers suggest patterns that can be created from their own range.

Paving slabs don't have to be rectangular; hexagonal ones are widely available.

Don't forget...

Bricks have dimensions that allow for mortar joints in between them, so don't expect to be able to lay them like close-fitting clay pavers. For most laying patterns you will need to bed the bricks on mortar, and mortar the joints between them.

Crazy paving

You can use broken paving slabs for this, which in theory reduces the cost. It's true that broken slabs may be cheaper, but you'll probably use more mortar and spend a lot more time on construction. And it's difficult to achieve a pleasing appearance with broken rectangular slabs.

Natural stone is a far better choice for crazy paving. For details on using natural stone, see the companion book to this one: *Stonework*.

The question of colour

Don't try to match the colour of your house walls too closely. If you get a good match, a large area of paving will look boring. If it's a near miss, it will probably look wrong. Matching colours work best if they're separated by flower beds, or perhaps a lawn.

If you want to harmonise with the house, choose a lighter or darker shade than the walls. Don't try to be too smart and match your paintwork. You'll probably want to repaint long before you think of changing the paving!

Grey is a neutral colour that you can use safely near any wall.

Below is just a small selection of bricks and pavers suitable for paths, drives and patios. It shows both the similarities and differences between bricks and clay pavers. Those in the middle column, and the brighter 'red' ones on the left, are all clay pavers; the others are bricks.

Look at the different dimensions and the thinner profile of the 'red' paver when compared with the brick above (which is designed to have mortared joints). The pavers in the middle column show the bevelled top edge that is usually a feature of pavers. The ones at the top have an indentation that gives the impression of smaller square blocks.

Choosing walling

Walls can be decorative as well as functional, and the choice of material makes a vital difference to the finished appearance.

For a boundary wall, bricks are still a popular choice, but decorative concrete blocks are widely used for internal walls and raised beds. Some of these bear a reasonable resemblance to natural stone. Others don't even pretend to be anything other than concrete blocks — but even they can look just right in a suitable setting where formal concrete slabs have been used for the paving.

Bricks

Compared with concrete blocks, bricks are light and easy to handle when you're laying them. But there are many different kinds, and it's worth visiting several builders' merchants before you make your choice.

Check that they're suitable for garden walls. And when you're working out how many you need, do bear in mind that you may need strengthening piers for a tall or a long wall.

You may also need coping to give the wall a neat finish. You can use bricks for this, but special coping blocks are better.

Keep on the legal side

Check that what you've planned is in keeping with the building regulations. In the UK, if you want to build a wall more than 1 m (3 ft 3 in) high adjoining a highway, or more than 2 m (6 ft 6 in) high anywhere else, you should check with your local authority first. In other countries, regulations will be different.

Concrete walling blocks

The most basic concrete walling blocks are cheap and cheerful, and won't win any awards in the design stakes. But many are attractively faced to resemble natural stone.

If blocks in the same range are available in several different sizes, then you'll be able to build a more interesting wall by incorporating the occasional larger block. This technique is commonly used with natural stone.

Some blocks look like several blocks already mortared together. This seems a quick and easy way to build a wall, but the down side is that they're that much heavier to work with than individual blocks, and they seldom look as convincing as a wall that has been assembled from individual blocks.

A concrete block wall, even one that looks like natural stone, will need some form of coping to look good.

Pierced (screen block) walling

This kind of walling block makes no apology for being concrete. It makes a virtue of the fact, and being rectangular and symmetrical it gives the wall a very distinctive appearance.

Instead of being solid, most pierced walling blocks have attractive designs that allow plenty of light and air to pass through, and this makes a high wall less oppressive. However, if you want privacy you may need to plant shrubs in front of the wall on one side.

These screen blocks are sometimes used for boundary walls, but they also make attractive screens or visual breaks for modern patios.

Although they're often mortared in position, walling blocks like these can also be 'glued' together with a special adhesive applied with a spreading tool.

Bricks or walling blocks?

The materials most commonly used for garden walls are bricks and walling blocks. Walling blocks come in many shapes and sizes, and vary greatly in finish, but bear in mind that large ones can be heavy to handle. Small walling blocks like the one in the picture are easy and convenient to handle.

Bricks also come in many forms. The two in the picture are pierced with holes; others have an indentation (frog) in the top or bottom. But always remember that you can't tell just by looking at them how suitable they will be for use in the garden.

The two bricks in the picture may look very similar to an untrained eye — but they're not. The one on the right is an engineering brick: it's very strong, it's water-resistant, and it can even be used as a damp-proof course for your wall. The one on the left is a 'common' brick that may be fine for house walls, but is rather less suitable for garden walls and raised beds.

Two bricks pierced with holes (top) and a small walling block (bottom) — both are easy and convenient to handle. Some bricks have an indentation (frog) in the top or bottom face.

Whenever you buy bricks, you should always explain what you want to do with them, and ask whether the ones you like are suitable.

Bedding on sand

If all that you want is an informal brick path that meanders along the garden, you can simply bed the bricks on sand (start by preparing the bed as shown in the panel). When you've finished you can point between the bricks with mortar to help prevent weeds becoming a problem.

For a stronger path, especially one that's likely to take regular or heavy traffic, bed them on mortar as shown on pages 18-19.

Don't forget that instead of bricks you can use clay pavers bedded on sand and vibrated into position (see pages 24-25), just as you can use bricks for a patio. Just make sure that you use the appropriate laying technique for your chosen material.

Preparing a bed of sand

Start by excavating the path to the anticipated depth of the bricks plus about 2 in (5 cm) to take the bed of sand or mortar.

For light use on stable ground, a bed of sand will be adequate on its own; but if you want extra stability without the labour involved in mixing a proper mortar base, you can sprinkle dry cement over the surface before laying the bricks. Chop it lightly into the sand with a trowel or spade. Moisture will seep through and help to form a solid base.

Laying the path

Lay the edge first, and then fill in the space between. A basket-weave pattern like the one shown here will look more interesting than bricks laid in straight rows.

After laying a short length of path, go over it to ensure the bricks are level. This will be easier if you use a straight-edged piece of timber cut to the width of the path to check the level, and then use the handle of a hammer or mallet to tamp down any bricks that are too high. If necessary, add a little more sand beneath any that are too low.

To stop weeds growing in the gaps between the bricks, it's best to fill the gaps with mortar. You can mix the mortar first, then fill the gaps with a pointing trowel.

However, for a small path, a quick and easy method may be adequate. Brush a dry mortar mix between the joints. Then use a small piece of wood, or a pencil on edge, to press the dry mortar down between the bricks and eliminate any large pockets of air. After that, brush over some more dry mix to top up any spaces.

Finally, water the path using a watering can fitted with a fine rose. Be careful not to flood the area or wash out the mortar — just moisten the surface (moisture will also seep up from beneath). If necessary, remove any mortar stains on the surface with a damp cloth before they dry.

Bedding on mortar

You may prefer to bed your brick path on mortar — one part cement to three parts soft sand, by volume. This will ensure that the structure remains firm even if the soil is unstable or the path has to take heavy traffic.

A bed of mortar is also advisable for the edging, especially if you're going to be using your bricks on end, or angled like the ones shown below. Even if you use modern concrete or imitation Victorian 'rope' edging, setting it in mortar will ensure it remains stable when you cultivate any beds beside the path.

Preparing the base

Don't mix too much mortar at once. Prepare just enough for a few yards (metres) of path, so that it remains workable without having to rush the laying.

Prepare a sub-base of rubble, gravel or compacted sand, about 3 in (8 cm) deep. Using a garden line, bed a length of edging on mortar, using a fillet of mortar behind each brick to help hold it in place. Then spread about 1 in (2.5 cm) of mortar over the compacted surface. Smooth it roughly, and lay the bricks with the frog (depression) down.

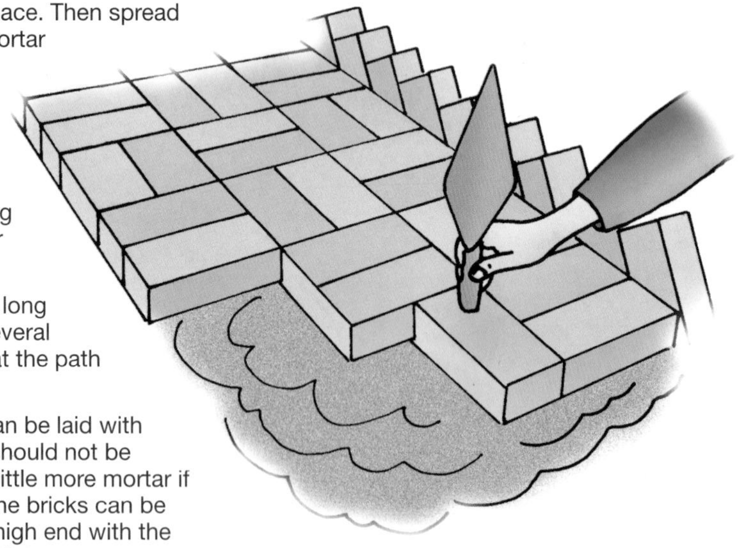

Tap the bricks level using the handle of a trowel or mallet.

Check frequently with a long spirit-level, using it in several directions, to ensure that the path is even.

If necessary, the path can be laid with a slope, but the bricks should not be uneven. You can add a little more mortar if necessary, but usually the bricks can be levelled by tapping the high end with the handle of a trowel or mallet.

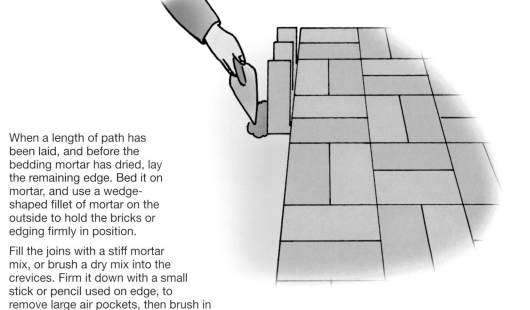

When a length of path has been laid, and before the bedding mortar has dried, lay the remaining edge. Bed it on mortar, and use a wedge-shaped fillet of mortar on the outside to hold the bricks or edging firmly in position.

Fill the joins with a stiff mortar mix, or brush a dry mix into the crevices. Firm it down with a small stick or pencil used on edge, to remove large air pockets, then brush in more mortar mix if necessary.

Sprinkle with water poured from a fine-rosed can, but avoid flooding the path. Aim to just moisten the mortar. Wipe off any stains before they are dry, using a damp cloth.

Paving a patio

You can use ordinary bricks for a patio, laying them in the same way as described for a path (see pages 16-19), but it's better to use clay pavers if you want the effect of bricks without the extra work involved in mortaring them. We show you how to lay a patio or drive with clay pavers on pages 24-25.

However, concrete paving slabs are a more popular choice for a patio or a large paved sitting area. As the picture on page 23 shows, paving slabs don't have to be boring, especially if you soften them with plants or mix them with other materials.

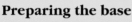

Preparing the base

There are many ways to lay paving slabs, but whichever method you choose you'll need to pre-pare the ground thoroughly if you want to avoid an uneven finish later.

If the area is currently lawn, simply remove the top 6 in (15 cm) of grass, and don't loosen the compacted soil under-neath. But if the ground has been culti-vated recently and is loose, compact it after you've dug it out to the required depth. Tread firmly with your feet, or tamp the ground with an improvised tool.

Add hardcore (rubble such as broken bricks and tiles) to a height that will allow for the depth of the paving slab. Allow an extra 0.5 in (12 mm) of mortar if it's only for foot traffic, and 1 in (25 mm) if it may sometimes have to support vehicles. Break up any large pieces of hardcore, and tamp to ensure that everything is consolidated.

Laying the slabs

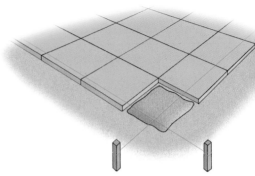

Start laying from one corner and work through to the opposite corner, using pegs and string as a guide to ensure that the edges are straight. If the paved area is going to take heavy traffic, lay the slabs on a solid bed of stiff mortar.

If the patio is for light use only, such as foot traffic and normal patio furniture, it's quicker and easier to use the spot-bedding method shown below (though it won't be as strong).

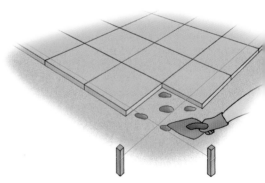

Use five blobs of mortar. Place one blob a short distance in from each corner, and one in the middle. Lower the slab into position, trying to ensure it's in the correct position.

Use the handle of a hammer or mallet to bed the slab evenly. Use a long spirit-level to check that each slab is flush with its neigh-bours, but be sure to allow for a slight fall so that water runs off freely.

Planning and preparation

Always lay paving with a slight fall in one direction so that rainwater runs off freely. If the patio or path is set against the house, make sure it slopes away from the building (see page 22). A gradient of 1:50 is adequate, even for a large area of paving.

It is essential that paving does not bridge the damp-proof course. The finished level should be 6 in (15 cm) below that level.

Unless the area is large, you needn't worry about the gentle fall when you're preparing a hardcore base. However, for a larger area of paving you may need to allow for the slope at this early stage.

Before starting to dig out the area, mark it out accurately with pegs and string.

Try to adjust the size so you won't have to cut any more slabs than absolutely necessary. Often you can't avoid cutting, but you may be able to use full slabs simply by reducing or enlarging the area a little. Don't forget to allow for mortar joints if the slabs require them.

Place the marker pegs a little way outside the area to be excavated, so they don't fall out while you're digging. (The place where the strings cross will indicate the corners.) When you're marking out, check that the corners are square, using a builder's square like the one described on page 9.

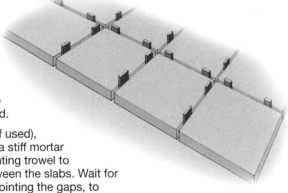

Unless the slabs are designed to butt-join (see previous illustrations), use home-made spacers (small, evenly cut pieces of wood) to ensure all the gaps are evenly spaced.

Remove the spacers (if used), then fill the joints with a stiff mortar mix, using a small pointing trowel to push it well down between the slabs. Wait for at least a day before pointing the gaps, to give the bedding mortar a chance to harden before you place your weight on the slabs.

For a sharper-looking, crisp finish, recess the joints slightly by pressing down with a suitably sized piece of wood (an old pencil might be suitable).

Brush and wipe off any surplus mortar from the slabs before it stains them.

Levels and slopes

If you like the idea of brick paving, but want the speed and convenience of laying paving slabs, these Burnt Brick antique paving slabs could be the answer. Each slab looks like twelve bricks laid in a basket-weave pattern.

It's usually necessary to lay paving with a slight slope in one direction, away from the house, to ensure that rainwater runs away freely.

There's a fairly simple way to ensure a level surface when preparing the ground. Use a spirit-level on a straight-edged piece of wood, spanning a series of pegs driven into the ground. Check the level from one peg to another in all directions, adjusting their height as necessary. Level the ground with the tops of the pegs.

Where you need a slight fall in order to avoid problems with standing water, you can still use a spirit-level on a straight-edge — but this time put a small wedge under the lower end of the straight-edge.

When you're laying the slabs, use the same wedge with your straight-edge and spirit-level in the direction of the fall.

How to cut a slab

Try to design your patio to a size and shape that avoids the need to cut slabs. This will avoid waste and make the job easier. Usually, however, it is necessary to cut at least a few slabs, perhaps to go around a step or maybe an existing flower bed.

If you have a lot of slabs to cut, it might be worth hiring a block splitter. Otherwise you can use the method below to cut them by hand.

Remember to wear protective goggles when scoring and cutting the slabs.

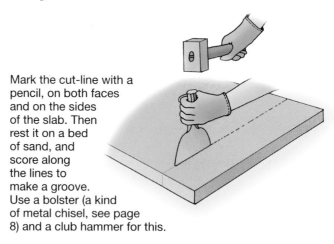

Mark the cut-line with a pencil, on both faces and on the sides of the slab. Then rest it on a bed of sand, and score along the lines to make a groove. Use a bolster (a kind of metal chisel, see page 8) and a club hammer for this.

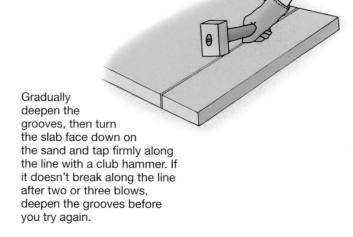

Gradually deepen the grooves, then turn the slab face down on the sand and tap firmly along the line with a club hammer. If it doesn't break along the line after two or three blows, deepen the grooves before you try again.

Clay and concrete pavers

Large slabs aren't always suitable for a patio or terrace, and smaller paving may be more appropriate. The brick-like appearance of clay pavers may also harmonise better with brick raised beds, and can tone in more sympathetically with house bricks, too.

Pavers made from concrete can also be used, and these are more attractive than they sound.

Pavers are meant to be bedded on sand, not mortared into place like bricks or paving slabs. Their close-fitting design means they can be held firmly in position simply by vibrating sand in between the joints.

Preparing a base

Excavate the soil to a depth of about 6 in (15 cm), and fix the edging in position. Special edging blocks are usually available from the manufacturer for edges not bounded by a wall, or you can use plain concrete path-edging blocks. Fix the blocks in position with fillets of mortar on the outside edge.

Instead of edging blocks you can use wooden battens secured in position — and in any case you'll need to fix a temporary wooden batten against existing walls, to support the board used to strike the sand level.

Fill the bottom of the excavated area with 4 in (10 cm) of compacted hardcore (rubble), with ballast (sand and shingle mix) worked in. This will ensure that there are no large air gaps where the sand layer will settle later on.

Cover the hardcore base with about 2.5 in (65 mm) of sand. This will settle to about 2 in (50 mm) when compressed. The sand for the base should be slightly moist: sprinkle a little water over it if necessary, but don't make it wet.

Clay pavers often blend particularly well with a house and garden.

Laying the pavers

Use a length of wood to compact and level the sand to the required height. Use the edgings or temporary supports to determine the correct height, making sure the pavers will be level with the edge when laid. If the paving is not too wide, use a length of wood with notches cut to the required depth to check this. If the area is too wide for this, insert temporary battens with their tops at the required depth, and use a straight-edged piece of wood over these.

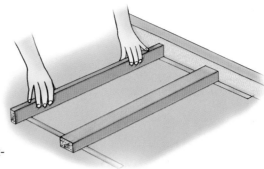

Lay the pavers in the pattern you've decided on, laying a couple of square yards (metres) at a time. With some laying patterns, such as the herring-bone style illustrated, you will have to cut some pavers to finish off the edges. This can be done with a block cutter (it's best to hire this), or with a bolster as described for paving slabs on page 22.

Use a kneeling board to work from, and butt the pavers closely. Tap them into place with the handle of a club hammer or a mallet, levelling them if necessary. Place a board across several pavers and use a mallet to ensure they are tamped level.

Brush dry fine sharp sand over the pavers, ensuring that as much as possible trickles between the joints. Repeat until no more sand seems to be accepted, then use a flat-plate vibrator to settle the sand between the joints. Brush in more sand, and vibrate again, repeating until the paving is stable and no more sand is accepted. If you can't hire a vibrator, you can use a board and mallet instead, but this is a more tedious method and not as satisfactory.

A rectangular bed

Raised beds add that extra vertical dimension, as important in a small garden as a large one. They also bring those colourful blooms that much nearer to eye level. The bed shown opposite replaced an area that had mostly been covered in grass in a small back garden, transforming it into something above the ordinary. Your raised bed doesn't have to be as large as this one. Just follow the basic steps described here, and adjust the dimensions to suit your own garden.

A firm foundation

All raised beds should be built on a firm foundation. If you're making a bed on an existing patio, you may be able to use the existing paving; but take out some of the paving slabs that will lie within the bed, and break up the soil to ensure that water can drain freely. If you're starting from scratch, it's important to lay a concrete bed, called a footing, on which the walls will be built.

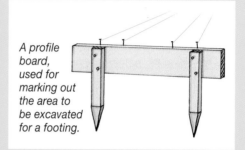

A profile board, used for marking out the area to be excavated for a footing.

Use profile boards (see illustration) made from 1-in (2.5-cm) timber nailed to small stakes that you can drive into the ground. Partially knock in four nails on the top of each board — space the inner ones to the width of the finished wall, and the outer ones to the width of the footing (concrete foundation). Drive the profile boards into the ground well outside the work area, so they won't become unstable when you dig out the trench.

Stretch string between the nails, to mark out the line of the walls. Then use a builder's square (see page 9) to check the corners are square. Measure diagonally across the corners as an additional check (both measurements should be the same). These basic but elementary checks are essential to ensure that the bed will be square.

Try to make sure that the length of each wall will make as much use as possible of full bricks, to avoid unnecessary cutting. Allow an additional 12 mm for mortar between each brick or walling block. As a check, lay a course of bricks loosely on the ground all around the bed, leaving mortar spaces, to make sure that your dimensions are correct.

Strictly rectangular beds are the easiest to build, but angled corners can look better, and they make it easier to walk around the bed. If you're angling the corners, set additional profile boards in the appropriate positions.

Temporarily remove the inner lines from your profile boards, then dig out the trench using the outer ones as a guide, and keeping the sides as vertical as possible. A wall up to 40 in (1 m) high will normally need a footing 4–6 in (10–15 cm) deep and 12 in (30 cm) wide. If you're laying a stronger wall that's two bricks thick, increase the depth to 9–12 in (23–30 cm) and the width to 18 in (45 cm).

Make sure your footing is level, or your final wall probably won't look right. Drive small wooden pegs into the ground at 3-ft (1-m) intervals, with their tops at the final level for the footing. Use a spirit-level to ensure they're all at the same height, then fill with a concrete mix to this level.

RAISED BEDS

A raised bed like this can become a focal point, even in a small garden. If you think angled corners will make it more difficult, just build a simple rectangle as in the step-by-step illustrations below.

Start by building up the corners in stepped tiers as shown. For advice on how to mortar and lay individual bricks, see pages 34–35.

Build the corners to the required height (five bricks, as illustrated, is about right for most raised beds).

Use a long spirit-level frequently to check the wall is absolutely vertical: place it diagonally across the corner as you lay each course to give an additional check. Take plenty of time over the corners, as it is essential that these are laid accurately.

With the corners laid, start filling in the spaces between them. Stretch a line between the corners (use pins and line; see page 8) to ensure that each course is straight and laid to the correct height. Lay the bricks loosely at first, to ensure even spacing, then begin to mortar them in (see pages 34–35). Lay them a course at a time, and work in from each end. Finish with a closing brick in the centre. Mortar both ends of this brick, and place a little mortar on the bricks either side, then position carefully, scraping off surplus mortar. Raise the builder's line when you lay the next course.

Ideally the wall should be capped with a coping to enhance its appearance and protect it from penetrating rain. Special coping blocks and bricks are available from builders' merchants, but you can use concrete slabs if these seem appropriate. The coping should overhang the wall a little to improve its appearance and help keep rain off the wall.

27

A circular bed

Even a small circular raised bed has a big visual impact — and it will probably stimulate more admiring comments about your DIY skills than a rectangular bed. It may look as though it's a more skilful job, but it needn't be any more difficult to build.

Marking out the excavation area

Before starting, you must first mark out the area to be excavated for the footing (foundation). Insert a peg in the ground where you want the centre of the circle to be, and loop a piece of string around it, with a stick or bottle filled with dry sand attached to the other looped end. Keeping the string taut, mark out the outer and inner extent of the footing by scribing with a stick or trickling sand out of the bottle.

Make the trench 18 in (45 cm) wide and about 6 in (15 cm) deep. To ensure the footing is level, insert pegs about 3 ft (1 m) apart; then use a spirit-level on a straight-edge to ensure that the tops of the pegs are all at the same height, which should be level with the top of the concrete.

Pour concrete into the trench, and level it with the tops of the pegs.

RAISED BEDS

Circular beds like the ones in the picture can look more stylish than rectangular beds of similar size, and are no more difficult to construct. Consider making several circular beds, and perhaps planting a tree in one of them.

Lay the bricks with a thicker wedge of mortar on the outer edge. You may have to add extra mortar to the outer edges as each course is laid.

It isn't practical to use the normal pegs and line to ensure that each course is level, so use the spirit-level all around the edge as each course is laid. Don't forget to check the vertical edge, too.

Use half bricks for the final course, or the edge may look too thick, especially on a small bed. If possible, use an angle grinder or block splitter to cut the bricks, as both ends of these cut bricks may be visible.

When filling the bed, take the soil over the lip that has been formed in this way. The effect of this will be to make the wall seem narrower than it really is.

Lay the bricks with their heads (ends) exposed, or it will be difficult to achieve a curve without very thick mortar joints. Lay a circle of bricks loosely first, to ensure that you can make a relatively smooth curve without excessively large wedges of mortar on the outside. You may have to remove or add a brick and readjust them. When they look right, draw around the inner and outer circles with chalk, as a guide for laying.

Interlocking beds

If you have a lot of individual rectangular raised beds dotted around the garden, they can easily look boring or even irritating. It's much more interesting to build a group of interlocking beds, like the one shown below.

A feature like this one will look far more interesting than three small free-standing beds. By building each section to a different height, you make the most of vertical space. And there's also another benefit: foliage and flowers from plants in the lowest beds help to mask some of the brickwork of the taller beds, so you can afford a little extra height without the bricks looking too dominant.

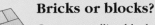

Bricks or blocks?

Concrete walling blocks may look incongruous against some backgrounds. If they do, then brick is a good choice for this kind of feature. But if it forms part of a modern patio, for example, you may prefer to use walling blocks (see pages 32-33), adjusting the dimensions accordingly.

Three beds that interlock will almost certainly look more pleasing than three separate raised beds. Such a feature makes a stronger focal point, but it's still a practical project for a novice bricklayer.

Prepare a footing (see description on pages 26–27). Although interlocking beds will have a more complicated shape than the one described there, the principle is the same. Just use a series of profile boards and strings to mark out each of the walls, allowing the strings to cross where necessary.

Build the bed according to the colour coding in the drawing. Start with the bed represented by light-coloured bricks, building it to a height of eight bricks. Use a simple running bond.

Then add the bed shown in brown, to a height of five bricks (you will have to cut a brick in half to complete some of the courses).

Finally, construct the bed of greenish bricks, this time to a height of just four bricks.

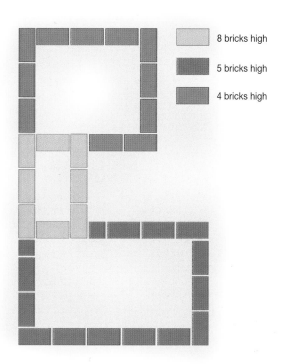

8 bricks high

5 bricks high

4 bricks high

Frogs and holes

Some bricks are made with a frog (depression) in one side, while others have a number of circular holes. This isn't just to make them lighter: it actually makes the bond stronger, because it allows the mortar to extend into the bricks as well as between them when they are pressed into position.

If you're using bricks with holes through them, you'll have to use coping (or a different kind of brick, without holes) for the final course. Bricks with frogs are usually laid with the frog upwards, but make sure the frog faces downwards for the final row unless you're using coping.

Know your bricks

Don't be tempted to buy inexpensive bricks intended for inside walls: they're not designed to withstand water penetration followed by freezing. Even ordinary bricks suitable for the external wall of a house may not be tough enough for a raised bed. After all, it'll be in contact with damp soil on one side and exposed to rain on the other.

You can buy special-quality bricks fired to withstand severe water and weather exposure. So it's best to explain to the builders' merchant exactly what you need them for, and check that they are suitable for a raised bed.

Building with blocks

Bricks aren't always the most appropriate material for a raised bed. Sometimes concrete walling blocks may look better in a particular setting. Although concrete sounds like a harsh garden material, many walling blocks resemble real stone; once they've weathered they can blend in very well with most garden settings. The feature shown in the picture shows just how pleasing concrete can be.

Buying your blocks

You'll find a bewildering array of walling blocks when you look around, and coming up with the right choice is far more difficult than choosing an appropriate brick. It helps to know that all of them are suitable for garden walls and raised beds, but there are far more patterns, shapes, textures and colours to consider.

Don't decide after visiting just one garden centre, as this will probably stock only a limited range of what's available. Visit several garden centres and builders' merchants, and send off for mail-order catalogues. Some of the manufacturers provide very helpful and inspirational catalogues that are packed with good ideas.

Different options

This project involves a simple flower bed, but you could also create a raised pond with a

Practical considerations

Walling blocks are generally larger than bricks, which means construction is often quicker — but don't make this a reason to choose the largest blocks unless you're sure you can handle them easily. Concrete blocks are heavy to work with.

Some concrete blocks have designs that make them look as though they're made up of a number of smaller pieces. Laying one of these will be quicker than laying perhaps half a dozen or more smaller blocks. On the other hand it will be much heavier to handle, and these larger blocks are less flexible when it comes to the size of your bed. It's difficult to cut them neatly, so it's sensible to make your bed a size that uses only full blocks.

This pleasing raised bed is made from concrete blocks, but from a distance it looks very much like real stone. You can fill it with soil and use it as a flower bed (as here), or incorporate a raised pond, leaving space for a flower bed around the edge. The step-by-step illustrations opposite show a different type of block with matching Ryedale coping (see panel top right), but the principle is essentially the same.

planting area around the edge and planting pockets in the side. If you want to include the pond, use a pond liner or a domestic water storage tank (you can easily excavate the ground within the bed to the required depth). For more information about raised ponds, including the incorporation of pond liners, see pages 60-65.

Coping

Concrete block walls often look unfinished unless they're topped with a suitable coping. A wide range of coping is available: most manufacturers offer a choice of different forms that harmonise with the types of walling they produce. Ryedale coping, for example, resembles the kind of stone you might find in a dry-stone wall built of natural materials.

Prepare a footing as for a brick raised bed (see pages 26–27). Build up the wall in courses to the required height, staggering the joints for strength. Manufacturers usually make blocks in a variety of sizes that allow this, yet still give flexibility in the size and design of your feature. Run a line along the length of the wall, as shown, to provide a guide when laying. Lay a bed of mortar about 0.5 in (12 mm) thick, trimming off surplus as the weight of the block squeezes some of it out at the sides.

Mortar one end of a block before laying, and use the handle of a club hammer or mallet to tap it level and firm it into position. Check visually against the line set up as a guide, but also use a spirit-level on every block. If you've chosen this kind of walling block, which resembles dry-stone walling, avoid conspicuous mortar joints, leaving them well recessed. Alternatively use a brick and tile adhesive (see page 42).

33

How to lay bricks

Bricklaying is a skill that has to be acquired, but it's worth the effort. Building walls can be extremely satisfying, especially as you watch them grow. There are just a few basic steps to learn, but it's worth practising with a few spare bricks first, to get the hang of applying the mortar and laying them level.

Pointing principles

Your brickwork will look much more professional if you pay attention to the way the mortar is finished off (pointed). Professionals have several ways of producing a smart finish, but the three most common methods are illustrated here:

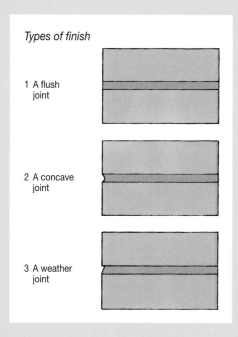

Types of finish

1 A flush joint

2 A concave joint

3 A weather joint

1 **Flush joints** have the mortar flush with the brickwork. You can achieve them simply by rubbing a piece of hessian or an old sack along the brickwork, creating a flush finish. It's quick and easy, but not as pleasing as the other finishes described in this panel.

2 **Concave joints** are quick and easy to produce, and look smart. You can buy inexpensive tools to make the job easier (one is shown on page 8), or you can improvise with a piece of bent tubing. Simply drag the tool along the joints, doing the vertical ones first, then going horizontally along the wall.

3 **Weather joints** take a little more time, but they're not difficult, and they're ideal for exposed positions where you want water to run off freely. Use a small pointing trowel to create this type of finish, angling the trowel to produce the joint, then trimming off any surplus that's been squeezed out.

Make sure the mortar is not too runny or too stiff for pointing. If you press a thumb into a mortared joint it should leave an impression of your thumb without the mortar sticking to your skin.

Scoop a measure of mortar, mixed to a stiff consistency, onto a bricklaying trowel: slide the blade under one edge of the heap, and use a flick of the wrist to flip it onto the trowel. Then deposit it in a ribbon on the course you have just laid, aligning the edge of the trowel along the centre of the bricks. To help spread the mortar along the bricks, draw the trowel towards you as you tip it.

Spread and furrow the ribbon of mortar by making a series of ripples as you move the point of the trowel along.

'Butter' one end of the brick to be laid, aiming to produce a neat layer about 0.4 in (10 mm) thick. Then press the brick against the one already in position, firming gently to level the brick with your string guide. This will ensure an even thickness of mortar.

When you're positioning and levelling the brick, surplus mortar may ooze from the sides. Remove it by running the edge of the trowel over the joint.

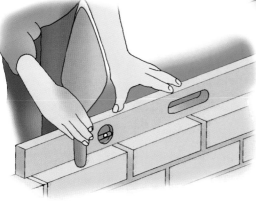

Use a spirit-level frequently to check both horizontal and vertical alignment. Get into the habit of checking whenever you've laid three bricks. Simply tapping them with the handle of the trowel is usually enough to ensure correct alignment.

Building a low boundary wall

High boundary walls are jobs for professionals or people with a lot of experience, but a low one is well within the capabilities of most of us. A wall may cost more than a hedge to start with, but you'll have no routine maintenance, it will probably let more light into your garden, and it will take up less of your valuable garden space than a hedge.

What's involved?

Building a low garden wall is similar in principle to making a raised bed (see pages 26–27), but you'll need piers at each end. If the wall is above a certain height, you'll also need to add strengthening piers at intervals. Any wall only a single brick wide (as in our example here) will benefit from piers, whatever its height. Double-brick walls are more substantial, but they take twice as many bricks, which means they cost a lot more. A low wall with a single thickness is an easier project for most beginners — although you may like to consider building a wall with a planting cavity.

Do I need piers?

Use the following as a guide to the piers you're going to need. It's a good idea to have piers even if the wall is lower than stated.

A single-thickness wall:
- maximum height without piers: 18 in (45 cm)
- maximum pier spacing: 10 ft (3 m).

A double-thickness wall:
- maximum height without piers: 4 ft 6 in (1.35 m);
- maximum pier spacing: 10 ft (3 m).

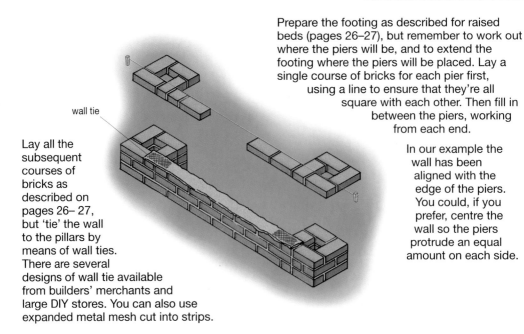

Prepare the footing as described for raised beds (pages 26–27), but remember to work out where the piers will be, and to extend the footing where the piers will be placed. Lay a single course of bricks for each pier first, using a line to ensure that they're all square with each other. Then fill in between the piers, working from each end.

In our example the wall has been aligned with the edge of the piers. You could, if you prefer, centre the wall so the piers protrude an equal amount on each side.

wall tie

Lay all the subsequent courses of bricks as described on pages 26–27, but 'tie' the wall to the pillars by means of wall ties. There are several designs of wall tie available from builders' merchants and large DIY stores. You can also use expanded metal mesh cut into strips.

You can use complicated, more decorative bonds for your wall; but the popular stretcher bond shown here is a sensible choice for a low, single-thickness wall. It's quick and easy for a beginner to lay.

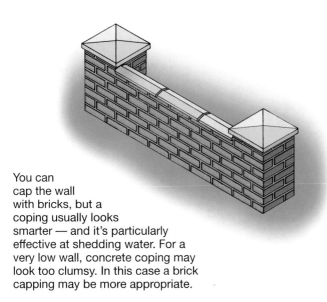

You can cap the wall with bricks, but a coping usually looks smarter — and it's particularly effective at shedding water. For a very low wall, concrete coping may look too clumsy. In this case a brick capping may be more appropriate.

Reinforcing rods

Piers taller than about 3 ft (1 m) should each be reinforced with an 0.7-in (16-mm) steel bar (available from builders' merchants and large DIY stores) concreted into position.

You'll need to set this in place when you lay the footing, so that the rod is firmly anchored in the base. Then build the pier around it and finally pour concrete into the cavity to encase the steel rod (for more details see pages 40–41).

Concrete boundary walls

Concrete walling blocks come in such a variety of colours and finishes that there's almost sure to be one that you find visually pleasing. Although large, plain blocks can look boring, there are plenty with attractive finishes, including some that can be used to create a 'random' finish. This kind of wall looks pleasantly informal. You can also introduce devices such as screen blocks within the solid walling blocks, to break up a wall that might otherwise look a little too oppressive or uninspiring.

If you're thinking of building a wall like the one shown below, which incorporates screen blocks, then be careful about the size of your walling blocks. Choose a size that will allow

Consider incorporating screening blocks into your concrete block wall. This can make a tall wall look less oppressive, and often enhances a low wall too.

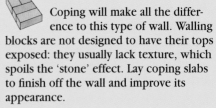

Coping

Coping will make all the difference to this type of wall. Walling blocks are not designed to have their tops exposed: they usually lack texture, which spoils the 'stone' effect. Lay coping slabs to finish off the wall and improve its appearance.

screen blocks to be incorporated easily. In this wall, for instance, the height of four courses of the main walling block equals the height of a single screen block. Study manufacturers' catalogues: they give all the essential dimensions.

Prepare a footing as described for brick walls (see pages 26-27), keeping the top slightly below the adjoining paving. Unless the wall turns and extends along the sides of the garden, remember to prepare a footing for brick or block pillars at each end. Try to make the wall a length that's a multiple of complete blocks. It will save you having to cut blocks, and will probably look better, too.

How to build

Use a line to ensure the blocks are laid straight and level, and bed the first course on a layer of mortar. Place only enough mortar to lay about five blocks. 'Butter' one end of each block with mortar, holding it on end and drawing the trowel downwards. Do this for the other end too, then position the block and tap into place.

Build up the ends or corners first, then lay the rest of the blocks up to the level where the screen blocks will be inserted.

Check for levels and verticals constantly, using a long spirit-level.

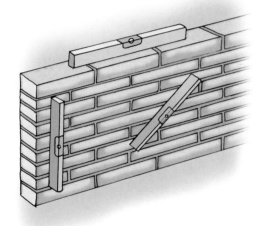

Lay a course to the point where your first screen block will go in, and then lay your screen blocks using the same thickness of mortar for the bed and between the blocks. Check the vertical spacing of the blocks (and adjust it if necessary) before continuing with the normal walling blocks.

weep holes

Screen block walls

Screen blocks (also called pierced blocks) are often used for internal walls within the garden. They can help to give a degree of privacy and shelter around the patio without 'shutting it in' like a solid wall. For much the same reason, screen blocks can also make very pleasing boundary walls.

If you're apprehensive about bricklaying, then the simplicity of building a screen block wall may very well appeal to you. You'll still need to be neat and methodical, and prepare a proper footing for your wall, but construction is gratifyingly fast, and the method of construction is very straightforward.

Laying screen blocks

Prepare a footing as described for brick walls (see pages 26–27), but making sure the trench is three times the width of the wall. Extend it by an additional 4 in (10 cm) at each end. When calculating the lengths, bear in mind that the mortar joints should be about 0.4 in (10 mm) thick.

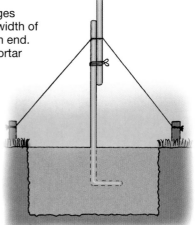

Before filling with concrete, make sure you mark the position of the pilasters (the pillars into which the blocks are slotted). You'll need to insert a steel reinforcing rod to run up the centre of each pilaster if the wall is more than 5 ft (1.5 m) high. Keep the rods upright while the mortar is setting by securing them with galvanised wire fixed to pegs. If you're building a high wall you may need to wire two or more rods together.

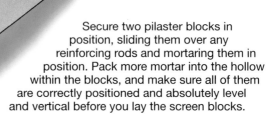

Secure two pilaster blocks in position, sliding them over any reinforcing rods and mortaring them in position. Pack more mortar into the hollow within the blocks, and make sure all of them are correctly positioned and absolutely level and vertical before you lay the screen blocks.

Place a 0.4-in (10-mm) bed of mortar on the concrete base between two pilasters, then lay the first course.

'Butter' one side of each block with mortar, making it about 0.4 in (10 mm) thick. Keep the mortar off the face of the block.

Position the first block by pushing it gently into the slot in the pilaster, and make sure it is both level and vertical.

Check alignment with a long spirit-level once you've laid a few blocks, and repeat each time you've laid another three or four blocks. It's usually easy to correct small irregularities simply by tapping on the top or side with the handle of your trowel. The line stretched above the pilaster blocks will also provide a visual guide.

Remember, though, that you can't lay to the actual line because the pilaster blocks don't align with the tops of the pierced blocks. This may seem odd, but it helps create a stronger wall.

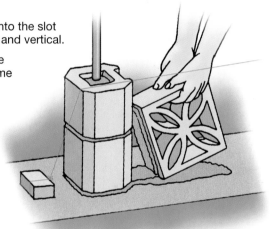

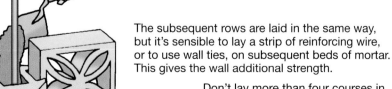

The subsequent rows are laid in the same way, but it's sensible to lay a strip of reinforcing wire, or to use wall ties, on subsequent beds of mortar. This gives the wall additional strength.

Don't lay more than four courses in a day. When you reach that height, leave overnight for the mortar to harden.

steps continue overleaf

Colour matching

Most screen blocks are white. If you don't like the darker colour of normal mortar, use a white masonry cement for the mortar. You may, however, prefer the contrast of a darker mortar, which emphasises the joints.

Right: *Screen blocks can be just as effective for boundary walls as they are for patio or internal garden walls, but they will look more substantial if they're laid on a base of bricks or walling blocks. If you're making a brick base you may prefer to build brick pillars instead of using pilasters.*

Finish off by mortaring the pilaster caps and wall coping into position, then rake the joints to produce a neat finish. Add more mortar if necessary.

Gluing them together!

If mortaring your wall together sounds like a messy and tedious chore, consider using an outdoor grade brick and tile adhesive for your walling blocks instead. You can use a cement-based walling adhesive that you apply with a spreader. As the joints will be thinner than those made with mortar, bear this in mind when calculating the spacing of your pilasters.

A loose-laid brick barbecue

Building a barbecue doesn't come easier than this — and you can be using it within hours of laying the first brick! If you have spare bricks left over from another project (you'll need 64), and you don't need a permanent barbecue, this is a fun project that you can probably finish in an hour.

Making the barbecue

Lay the first course of six bricks with the corners just touching. Then lay the second course in a similar way, but staggered (as shown) to span the gaps in the first course.

Lay nine courses, then place a metal sheet to form a hearth. Making this is the most difficult part of the job, but your local forge, garage or metalworker should be able to make one for you if you give them a template and explain what it's for. Then lay four bricks along the back, and two cut halves for the front, as shown, leaving a 9-in (23-cm) gap.

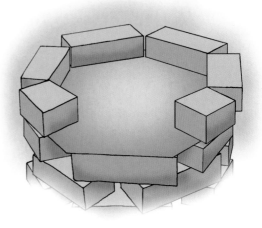

This temporary brick barbecue is quick and easy to make, especially if you have spare bricks left over from another project. It looks reasonably permanent, yet it's easy enough to dismantle and store at the end of the season.

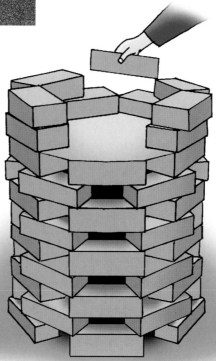

Place the next five bricks as shown in the drawing, then add a small grill (see picture above). You might be able to buy a grill from a garden centre that sells barbecues, though it may be difficult to find one the right size. If so, you could just use an old grill from a household cooker.

Finally, position four more bricks along the back and sides as in the picture above, which shows a loose-brick barbecue in use.

A built-in barbecue

Give your patio that professional look with a built-in barbecue. It's not difficult to build one like that shown on page 49, and you'll find it a gratifying as well as a practical project to complete.

Building the barbecue

First buy a grill set from a garden centre or a large DIY store. These sets are sold specifically for DIY barbecue projects and are readily available. Don't build your barbecue first and then try to find a grill kit that fits it!

Lay your blocks or bricks out on the paving around the grill (if you're not building on existing paving, you'll have to make a footing as described on page 26). Don't forget to allow spaces for the mortar joints. If you do your homework first, you should be able to avoid cutting too many blocks or bricks.

Draw a chalk mark around the provisionally placed blocks or bricks, and then place a bed of mortar about 0.5 in (12 mm) thick within these lines as you lay each side (see next illustration).

Blocks or bricks?

Whether you use walling blocks or bricks is a matter of personal preference — the principles of construction are the same. Much depends on having an appropriate surround.

If you choose walling blocks, you'll probably find it easier to use small blocks similar to the ones in the picture on page 49, but you can use larger and more complex blocks if you prefer.

Lay the first row of slabs or
bricks (see above), 'buttering' one end of
each slab or brick with mortar (see below
right). Firm each one into place by gently
tapping it with the trowel, then trimming off
surplus mortar.

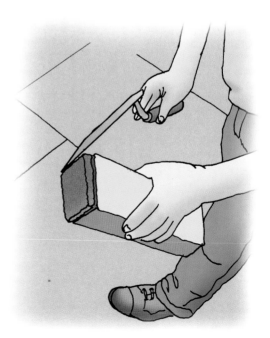

steps continue overleaf

47

Use a spirit-level frequently to ensure that the blocks are level. Once the second course has been laid, check that they are straight vertically, too. If they're just a little out of alignment, a gentle tap with the handle of a club hammer or mallet is usually all that's needed.

When you've laid about six courses, use blocks crossways to form a lip on which the grate will rest. A paving slab can also be supported — this will make a small preparation or serving table (see picture opposite). You may have to cut these blocks to size, as full blocks will probably be too long (see panel opposite).

Continue with one more course all round, then extend the barbecue section by a further two courses. Again use blocks cut crossways to form a support, this time for the grill. Finish off with a final course of bricks or blocks.

Cutting and pointing

A block splitter is useful for cutting the walling blocks or bricks required to fit a particular space, or to form a supporting lip.

Alternatively you can cut them with a club hammer and bolster chisel as described for paving slabs and bricks (see page 22). However, it's more difficult to achieve a clean and even break.

Your barbecue will need pointing to produce a smart, mortared finish between the blocks or bricks. Use any of the techniques described on page 34.

Brick or walling block barbecues are simple to make, yet they give that finishing touch to a patio which makes it look really well designed.

A retaining bank

If you garden on a slope, you may need a retaining bank to stop soil from washing away after heavy rain, or to provide terraces of flat ground to garden on. Even quite modest slopes may need a retaining wall. These have to be substantial enough to hold back the soil, even when the pressure is increased by heavy rain.

A wall intended for only a small bed can be just one brick wide, but a retaining wall has to be stronger than that, because it's likely to be subject to greater pressures. In fact it should normally be two bricks wide, which is about 8.5 in (215 mm).

It's also a good idea to incorporate weep holes (gaps where water can drain through) along the bottom to avoid either waterlogging or a build-up of pressure after heavy rain. A practical bonding pattern (known as an 'English bond') is the one that has been chosen for illustration here, for reasons that will become clear.

An English bond wall

The low boundary walls and raised beds described earlier in the book were built with a pattern of bricks known as a 'running bond'. If this bond were used in a double brick wall there would be a weak vertical joint between the two rows of bricks, so the English bond is used instead. It's stronger because alternate courses are laid in opposite directions.

Weep holes

To allow surplus water to drain from behind a retaining wall, and avoid a build-up that will put pressure on it, you should leave out a header brick at the bottom of the wall every couple of yards (metres). Mortar a length of drainage pipe in its place.

To avoid the 'weep hole' becoming clogged, pack plenty of rubble and gravel behind it to help the soil drain freely.

You will, unfortunately, have to cut a few bricks in half lengthways to insert before the last 'header' brick in each row (see illustrations opposite). The footing should also be more generous: twice the width of the wall, and deep enough to go below the frost line. Use the basic bricklaying techniques described on pages 34-35, but follow the guidelines opposite for the bonding pattern and the laying sequence at the corners.

A retaining bank may in practice be essential on a sloping site, and sometimes replaces what might be an ordinary garden wall in a level garden — but it can also have the advantage of bringing small plants that much closer to eye level!

Coming to terms

Bricklayers may often use terms that are unfamiliar to most of us, but they're easy to learn. Below are the terms used in laying an English bond wall — you'll find further bricklaying terms explained in the glossary on pages 76-79.

- **Header face** refers to the small end of the brick.

- **Stretcher face** refers to the long side of the brick. In the wall illustrated you can see alternate rows of exposed header and stretcher faces.

- **Queen closer** is a term sometimes used to describe a brick cut in half lengthways (see the inset in the first illustration opposite).

An English bond wall

Cut a few bricks lengthways (making queen closers) to close the gaps created at the ends of the wall turns. Lay the first course in the sequence indicated. Every second course will be laid to the same pattern.

Lay the second course — and every even-numbered course — in the sequence illustrated here, again using half-bricks to close the gap as shown.

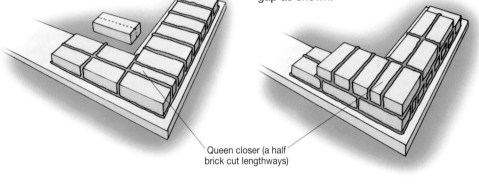

Queen closer (a half brick cut lengthways)

Making a terrace

Terraces can transform a slope that is difficult to cultivate into a series of level and interesting areas with lots of gardening potential. And if you choose an attractive walling material, the whole feature will enhance your garden.

Terracing principles

If you're planning to create a terrace, be prepared for some hard work! It's not so much the construction of the walls that's labour-intensive as the physical levelling of the ground to produce flat areas. You'll need to slice into the bank on one side of the wall and deposit the soil on the other side (see illustration opposite).

There's also the question of topsoil. Unless you first remove the top 9-12 in (23-30 cm) of soil and place it to one side to be returned to the surface after levelling, you'll end up with impoverished and infertile soil on the surface.

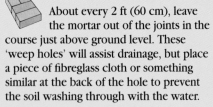

Weep holes

About every 2 ft (60 cm), leave the mortar out of the joints in the course just above ground level. These 'weep holes' will assist drainage, but place a piece of fibreglass cloth or something similar at the back of the hole to prevent the soil washing through with the water.

If you intend to pave the whole area, it doesn't matter, but it's a major problem if you want to create flower beds.

Bricks can be used for the retaining walls, but if there's a series of terraces you may find that brick looks a bit boring from the lower levels. Many concrete walling blocks are attractive, and those that resemble natural stone can look particularly pleasing.

For advice on the preparation of the footing, and how to lay walling blocks, see pages 26-27 and 32-33.

To form a level terrace on a sloping site, cut into the bank as shown, using the earth that you dig out to raise the level of the ground behind the position of the retaining wall. You'll need to extend the area you cut into far enough to allow for the construction of the wall, backfilling afterwards.

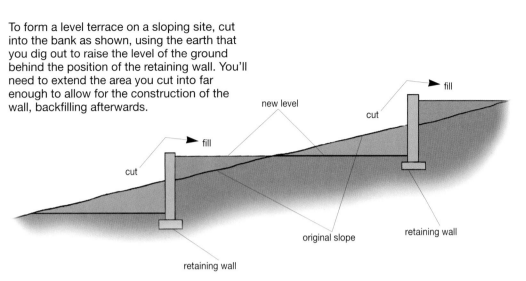

Build the wall on a footing at least three times the width of the wall, with the top of it below the final ground level.

Don't backfill with soil without providing for drainage. As well as making a few weep holes (see panel), lay a perforated drainage pipe behind the wall, with a gradual slope to a large soakaway or a drainage system. Pack a generous amount of rubble and gravel behind the wall and around the pipe, then top up with soil.

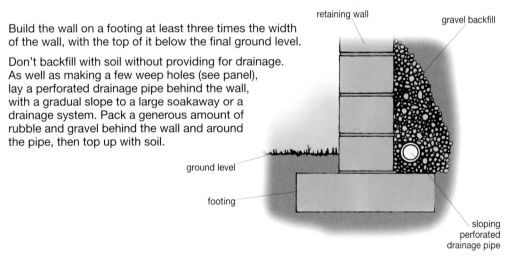

Left: *Walling blocks make strong and attractive retaining walls for terraced ground. You'll have to link the terraces with paths or steps, but try to avoid too many rigid straight lines. This retaining wall, for example, has been made more interesting by curving the end where it meets some steps to the next level.*

Stepping up

Steps can be either complicated or easy to make, depending on their design and the materials you use. The easiest are straight steps that use bricks or small concrete walling blocks for the risers and paving slabs for the treads.

Terms explained

The **riser** is the vertical distance from one step to the next. About 6 in (15 cm) makes the climb comfortable, but if the slope is steep you may have to increase this.

The **tread** is the horizontal distance from the front to the back of the step, including any overhang.

For the ideal dimensions, follow the advice given on page 56.

Helpful guidelines

Whenever possible, make your steps wide enough to use complete paving slabs. Cutting them is troublesome, and the joints never look so neat.

It's also a good idea to make the steps shallow, perhaps two bricks high. This makes them visually more pleasing than steep steps, and easier to use.

Before excavating, measure the difference in height between the top and bottom of the slope, and calculate approximately the number of steps and the position of each. Mark the position of each step with pegs, which you can easily adjust if necessary.

Using your pegs as a guide, dig out the soil to the approximate size and shape of the steps. This doesn't have to be exact as further adjustments will be necessary later.

Start laying the steps by preparing a footing for the first step. This should be made from 4–6 in (10–15 cm) of concrete over a base of compacted hardcore.

Lay the bricks for the risers. For light use, a running bond just one brick wide should be enough.

If you want to be sure of greater strength and stability, make the support wider by laying a double row of bricks with the stretcher (long) face parallel to the slabs. Top this with a second row laid the opposite way round, with the headers (short ends) facing outwards.

step-by-step description continues overleaf

Backfill with rubble such as hardcore, or ballast (a mixture of gravel and sand), to the level of the bricks. Then mortar the slabs into position, overlapping the edge by about 1 in (2.5 cm). This gives a crisper-looking edge to the steps.

Measure in from the edge of the slab and mark the position for the next row of bricks for the riser (these should be laid on the previous tread). Lay a bed of mortar and position the bricks. Then repeat the process to the top of the flight.

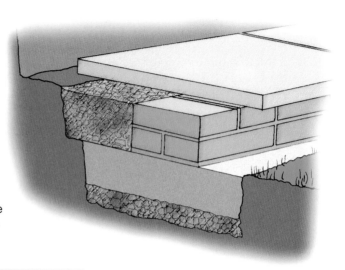

Ideal dimensions

Your flight of steps may be long or short — that's dictated by the slope. But apart from this you can control the dimensions; and it's a good idea to aim for those that experience has shown are easy to use and easy on the eye.

- **Risers**
  A good height for the riser is about 6 in (15 cm), with a tread of about 15 in (38 cm). This isn't always possible, though, and indeed it may not be appropriate for a particular situation. For comfort, try to make the riser at least 4 in (10 cm) high, and not more than 7 in (16.5 cm).

- **Treads**
  Treads should not be less than 11 in (28 cm) deep for comfort. The stairs in your home may be less than this, but everyone knows how difficult they can be to climb.

Steps are practical features for a sloping garden, but changes of level and a few steps are useful design features even if you start with a level site. There are many ways to make steps, and many materials to choose from, but a combination of bricks for the risers and paving slabs for the treads can look smart, and construction is uncomplicated.

An alternative method

If you're using walling blocks for raised beds or retaining walls, and you want to build steps nearby, then they may look better if you use the same type of block for the risers. This will give your design a more integrated appearance. Most walling manufacturers make paving slabs that harmonise with your walling blocks, and if you choose these for the treads it will help your steps to blend in.

You can make your steps using the same method as that described for brick risers (see pages 54-57), but the steps below show a variation that you could also use.

Prepare a concrete footing for the first step, as described on page 54, and then build the steps in a similar way to that described earlier.

Work out whether you need to use one or two blocks for the riser. You can do this provisionally with pencil and paper once you know the height of the slope. Then excavate the steps, using pegs and string to indicate the position of each one. Don't

How wide?

Don't ever make your steps too narrow. If they're only the width of a single paving slab they'll look mean and be difficult to negotiate. Go for a width of at least two paving slabs — or about 2-3 ft (60-90 cm) depending on slab size.

If there's room to extend the width by a further paving slab, it will be easy for a couple to negotiate the steps side by side rather than in single file.

forget that instead of starting with a riser, you could lay a tread into the slope to start off the first step; this gives you more flexibility in your calculations. You can also cut the steps into the bank, or build them up above the surrounding soil on either side.

Walling blocks are likely to make more appealing risers for your steps if they match or blend with surrounding walling blocks. It's usually possible to choose matching paving for the treads. On the other hand, you can create an even more individual effect by making crazy-paving steps using broken slabs.

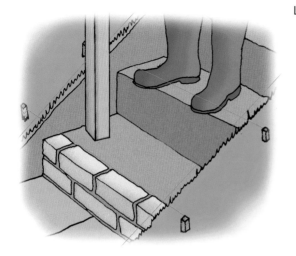

Lay your walling blocks one or two high, depending on the height you want to achieve and the size of the block. Unlike bricks, walling blocks vary in size. Backfill with compacted hardcore and gravel, or compacted ballast (gravel and sand), to provide a firm base on which to lay the slabs.

Finishing touches

Don't forget to point the joints with mortar to produce a neat finish and prevent weeds gaining a foothold. Some popular pointing finishes are illustrated on page 34. Of these, a flush joint is simple and effective both for paving slabs and for bricks or walling blocks.

If you cut your steps into the slope — rather than building them with the treads just above the surrounding soil — you may have a problem at the sides unless you retain the soil in some way.

One solution is to build small retaining walls at the sides. Alternatively you can cut back the soil so it slopes gently towards the steps, then plant with compact, ground-hugging shrubs that will stabilise the soil and mask the edge.

When you are building a patio, you can sometimes lay paving slabs on five blobs of mortar. For steps it's best to lay a ribbon of mortar around the edge. For additional strength you can also lay a cross of mortar in the middle.

Press the slab into position, tapping it level if necessary. Use a spirit-level to check that the slabs are even, and aligned across the path. It doesn't matter if there is a very slight fall towards the edge, as this will help to shed rainwater more easily.

Don't forget to overlap the slab over the riser by up to 1 in (2.5 cm).

A raised patio pond

A raised pond will bring the wonderful world of
the underwater that much closer to eye level —
and it's easier to make friends with your fish
when you don't have to stoop! A raised pond
also makes a stronger visual feature than the
more conventional sunken pond. If you can
build a simple brick or block wall, you'll find
this a relatively easy project to complete.

A rectangular construction

Build your brick or block walls as if you were
constructing a raised bed (see pages 26-27) —
but if you're using bricks, make the walls two
bricks wide. If you're using substantial concrete
blocks, a single thickness should be enough to
withstand the pressure from a small pond.

Be sure to build the wall on a concrete footing
(see page 26). If you're planning to render the
inside with mortar, either lay a concrete base
over the whole area, or prepare the footing
first, and then lay a concrete base within it.

Prepare a layer of compacted hardcore before
you lay the concrete base. Break large pieces
up with a sledgehammer or club hammer, to
provide a reasonably level and firm
base before pouring the concrete.

Cover the hardcore with at least
1 in (2.5 cm) of concrete. Tamp
and level this roughly, using a
chopping motion with a shovel.

Make sure it's waterproof

A rendered pond needs an
additional waterproof coating, even if you
added a waterproofing product to the
concrete and render. Water will find the
smallest crack or weak point to seep
through, so it's worth the extra cost and
effort to apply a sealer.

You can use a resin pond waterproofer or
a bitumen-type paint intended for ponds.
The latter is easier to use and usually
cheaper; the resin is likely to give a
longer-lasting seal.

Follow the manufacturer's instructions
for applying the resin very carefully. A
waterproof pond paint like the one
illustrated on page 62 is easily applied
with a brush. It may look brown when
you apply it, but will dry black. Several
coats are advisable.

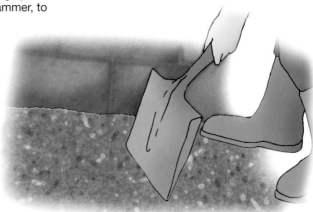

When the base concrete has set, render it with mortar to which a waterproofing product has been added. Use a float trowel to pro-duce a smooth surface. It doesn't matter if it's not exactly level. Any slight unevenness won't be noticed once the pond has been filled with water, but it's important to produce a good seal all round. Repeat the process once the first render has set, to ensure a waterproof seal at the base and edges.

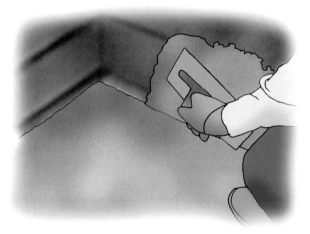

When applying the second render to the base, take the mortar mix up the sides as you work, applying a coat at least 0.2 in (6 mm) thick. If the mortar won't adhere to the sides easily, moisten the bricks or blocks with a damp brush first.

Don't forget to add a waterproofing product, or your pond is likely to leak. You can obtain these from any good builders' merchant, large DIY store or water-garden specialist.

steps continue overleaf

Leave the render to dry out for several days, then apply a waterproof coating. Special bitumen-based paints intended for pond use are readily available and easy to apply with a brush. Be sure to cover all the inner surfaces, paying special attention to corners and crevices. The water will soon find them if you don't!

Apply at least two coats.

Walling blocks make a quick and easy raised pond. Waterproof your pond with a pond liner, or render the inside with mortar and then coat it with pond resin or waterproof pond paint.

Using a liner

If rendering and sealing the inside of your raised pond seems tiring and time-consuming, you can use a pond liner instead. This will have to be applied before the wall has its coping, as you need to fold and trim the liner so it overlaps the edge of the bricks or blocks by about half their width. The coping can then be mortared into position, trapping the liner and hiding the cut edge. Your pond will then be waterproof up to the level of the coping.

You'll have to pleat the liner at the corners. At first this will look somewhat unattractive, but the pressure of the water will hold the pleats against the sides once the pond has been filled. And if you use a black liner they won't be conspicuous.

You'll need to protect the liner from sharp edges on the walls, and to provide additional insulation for the pond (raised ponds are more likely to freeze than those below ground). To do this, cut sheets of expanded polystyrene to fit around the walls.

Pleat the liner at the corners and fold the top over the wall so it can be trapped when the coping is mortared into position.

Curved and complex

A curved pond usually looks more 'designed' and professional than a simple rectangular pond, especially if it's cleverly integrated into the rest of the garden like the one illustrated below. It won't be as easy to build as the pond on the previous pages, but it should have much more impact.

Although small concrete blocks can be used for circular and curved ponds, you'll probably find bricks easier to work with. You can render and waterproof the finished pond as described on the previous pages, but using a liner will be easier and more convenient.

A pond like this is an ambitious project unless you've built a few simple walls first, but it's well worth the effort. If you are able to incorporate your raised brick pond with other brickwork walls, the result will look really well planned.

Banking on a good impression

As can be seen from the picture below, a raised pond built into a bank can be particularly effective.

Building a raised pond in the centre of a flat area can look incongruous, but if it has a suitable backdrop — or better still if it links to a bank or some raised beds behind — it will have a far more 'designed' appearance. It will also give your raised pond a 'softer' look.

Prepare a footing as previously described for raised beds (see page 26), but modify the way you mark out the area to be excavated. This will involve scribing arcs in the ground using pegs and strings.

With the footing prepared, apply a bed of mortar for the first course, and mark the arc the bricks will be laid to, using the point of a trowel.

To determine the line for both footing and brickwork, loop a measuring tape or string around a peg fixed in a central position, and scribe your line with a stick held taut at the other end.

You may have to cut bricks to fit where a curve meets a straight wall or another curve. Otherwise build up the walls as you would a garden wall. It's advisable to use one of the bonds that makes a wall two bricks thick, such as the English bond described on pages 50–51. Build as far as the last course before the capping course.

When you've laid the penultimate course and the mortar has set, lay a 1–2-in (2.5–5-cm) thick bed of sand in the base to cushion the liner from stones and large roots. Then insert the flexible pond liner.

Fill the pond with water, pleating the liner where necessary. It may be more manageable if you cut it roughly to size, leaving a margin for trimming later. Don't attempt to trim it to its final size before filling, as it is difficult to calculate how far up the liner will come in a curved pond before it's filled.

When the pond is filled, trim to take the liner over the edge of the bricks, leaving enough to trap beneath the top course of bricks.

Pergola piers

With pergolas you can make the most of the many beautiful climbers that are just waiting to be grown, and they also add that vital vertical element to your garden. Most gardeners use rustic poles for a pergola, but if you make one from brick piers and sawn timber the impact will be that much greater — and your garden will have a stronger sense of design.

Build your pergola to a size that suits your garden. If your garden is small, don't make it too long or too large. On the other hand, if you have a large garden and want your pergola to

provide a focal point, then you can build a substantial structure. For more tips on the size of pergola, see the panel on page 68.

The step-by-step instructions given here show how to make a pergola pier from bricks, but if you wish you can use small concrete walling blocks instead. These may be more appropriate if your pergola links with a patio where concrete walling blocks have been used, or in a garden where there is extensive concrete paving. Brick is a better choice if you have a path or patio made of bricks or clay pavers.

How to assemble

Start by preparing a footing of concrete, at least 9 in (23 cm) thick, over a bed of hardcore. Make sure it will extend for at least 6 in (15 cm) beyond the extent of the brickwork.

Pergola pillars are tall, so the hollow cavity will be in need of some reinforcement. Use 0.7-in (16-mm) steel reinforcing bars (available from good builders' merchants), and set the bar in the concrete footing, as shown in the picture.

It may also be necessary to extend the reinforcing bar for a tall pillar. If so, then you should overlap the two bars by about 18 in (45 cm), and secure them together firmly with galvanised wire.

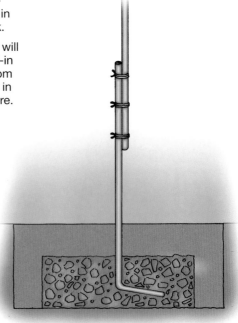

Use four bricks for each course, laying them in a simple bond as shown in the illustration. For advice on laying bricks, see pages 34–35. Be particularly conscientious about checking the vertical alignment with a spirit-level as each course is laid.

Every time you have laid another six courses of bricks, pour some concrete mix into the cavity, always making sure at the same time that the reinforcing rod remains vertical.

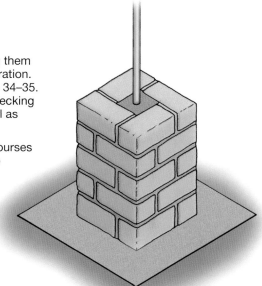

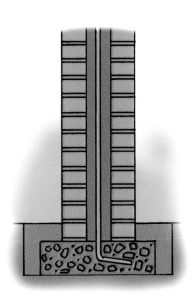

When the pier has been built to the height that you want, cap it with tiles or a small concrete slab. You can buy flat clay tiles that can be built into quite ornamental designs, but keep it simple unless you are confident about this.

You can use a small pier cap or small paving slab instead, and this is the best choice if you use walling blocks instead of bricks for the pillar. Whatever you cap the pillar with must be flat, to support the pergola timbers.

steps continue overleaf

Sizing up the problems

To look right, your pergola should have a width and height that are in proportion to each other, and that are also appropriate for your garden.

Ideally, your pergola should be wide enough for two people to walk through it side by side. Bear in mind that if you grow prickly plants like climbing or rambling roses, you need to allow for thorny stems growing out at the sides as well as hanging from the overheads.

The height should be at least 6 ft 6 in (2 m), or perhaps 1 ft (30 cm) higher if you plan to grow climbers over the crossbeams. Hanging, and especially thorny, stems can be a hazard if they're not tied in.

Seasoned hardwood makes a pergola like this very expensive, yet ordinary softwood is unlikely to last so well (it should always be treated with a preservative). The most practical option is Western red cedar, or a softwood impregnated with a preservative that is safe for use with plants.

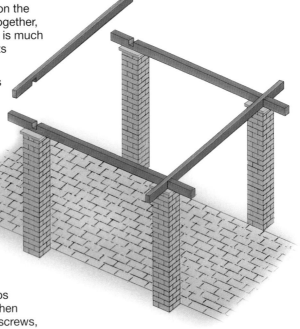

Cut and assemble the timber beams on the ground, without screwing any joints together, to make sure that everything fits. This is much easier than trying to make adjustments when working above head level.

The exact method of fixing the beams to the pillars will depend on your choice of capping. You may be able to mortar dowels or bolts into the concrete reinforcement, or even use the tip of the reinforcing rod, with a hole of appropriate size drilled in the beam to slip over it.

Otherwise secure the beams to the pillars with bolts set in mortar.

You should first secure the beams that run along the length of the pergola, ensuring that any joins are positioned over the pillar caps for additional strength and support. Then secure the crossbeams in place with screws, or galvanised nails driven in at an angle.

Right: *A pillared pergola not only makes an impressive garden feature, but provides the ideal support for climbers like this 'Maigold' rose.*

A well-decked garden

A neat finish

If you're using mortar, be careful not to let any of it deface the inside faces of the bricks. Later on you'll find it difficult to remove all traces of mortar in the inaccessible spaces between the bricks, so sponge off any marks before the mortar dries.

Your well will be surprisingly stable even if you don't use mortar.

A decorative 'well' makes a superb focal point, and isn't as difficult to make as you might think. You don't need to create a working windlass, for example — just something that suggests the various elements of an old-fashioned well.

If you want to, you can of course build an entirely convincing replica of an old well. But if you're simply making a focal point for a modern garden, rather than trying to recreate a cottage or period garden, it makes sense to keep things simple and to go for an overall impression rather than authentic detail.

We've described how to make the well shown below, but this is a project you should modify to suit your own garden and your own individual taste.

A project to be proud of — and it's not as difficult or complicated to build as it might appear. Simple carpentry and bricklaying skills are all you need.

Finishing touches

Wind a length of rope around the windlass, and hang a bucket or basket from it.

You can use a length of plastic rope like the one shown in the photograph, or for a more authentic effect you could buy a length of traditional rope.

Decide on the size of your well, and make the well-head just large enough for the uprights to fit inside the brick circle.

Cut the timber to size, following the basic pattern shown. You can use fence posts for the uprights, and improvise a windlass. For instance, you might be able to find a roller from an old mangle. If the windlass causes problems, leave it out.

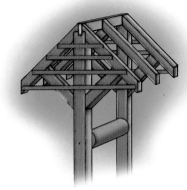

Concrete the uprights into the ground, at the same time as you prepare a footing for the wall (see pages 26–27 for details). Make the footing about 1 ft (30 cm) wide and 9 in (23 cm) deep. Although the bricks won't be mortared in the conventional way, it's important for them to be laid on a level and stable base.

Start by laying the first course of bricks loosely, to make sure they are spaced evenly around the edge. Then mortar the first row in position.

It's important that the bricks are close enough together to support the second row of bricks at the edge of the circumference (see illustration).

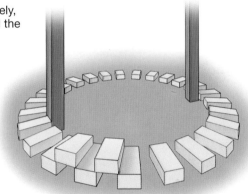

Lay about eleven courses, using a thin layer of mortar if you prefer, though for a neat effect like the one shown the mortar joints can be omitted.

Top the brickwork with cladding tiles; some of these will have to be cut to shape.

Lining the roof

Nail roof tiles to the battens, but use a little mortar on the edge tiles for extra security. If you want to tile the ends too, as shown in the photograph, fix battens into position and then nail more tiles in place (you will probably have to cut some of them to shape).

Finish off with ridge tiles, mortaring them into position.

Stepping stones

If your garden lawn looks a little uninteresting, then you could add a stepping-stone path. This is a quick and easy job that you can do in a day, and it can transform an otherwise boring part of the garden.

Spacing and pacing

Start by laying out your slabs on the surface, and adjust the spacing until they look right and feel right to walk on. The best spacing will depend on the size of the slabs and the length of your normal walking stride. They only have

to be too close or too far apart, and they'll soon become an irritation.

Once they look right, ask the other members of the family who are likely to use them most often to walk along the slabs. If the spacing seems comfortable while they're raised above the lawn, they'll certainly feel right once they're set into the grass — and by then it won't matter if you step over the edges slightly.

When you're perfectly happy with both appearance and comfort, lay the stepping stones as described opposite.

Leading somewhere

Stepping stones should always have a sense of purpose. Don't add them just for the sake of it: make sure they lead from one path to another, or perhaps to a garden shed or the greenhouse. If you have a sundial or birdbath somewhere in the lawn, you could have a curved stepping-stone path leading to it from one side. You could even extend the path beyond the feature and into another part of the garden; but use a circle of the same paving stones around the feature itself to make it look well designed.

If there's no obvious place for your path to go, then try extending the stepping stones into a border after they've crossed the lawn — perhaps to a seat, a statue or an ornament on a plinth.

Always bear in mind that your path doesn't have to run in a straight line: a gentle curve is often more pleasing. Try to avoid taking the path along the middle of the lawn, as this has the visual effect of cutting it in half.

Cut around the edge of each slab with a spade or a half-moon edger, to mark out the ground. Then place the slab to one side and lift the turf where it's going to be placed.

Excavate the ground to the depth of the slab plus about 1.5 in (4 cm). Place about 1 in (2.5 cm) of sharp sand in the base and bed the slab on this. The finished level of the slab should be about 0.2–0.5 in (6–12 mm) below the grass, so it doesn't interfere with mowing.

Left: Paving slabs don't have to be square. If the surrounding paving is formal and uses octagonal slabs, for example, these might look good for your stepping stones too. You can also use more than one size of rectangular slab to make a more positive statement, as shown in this picture. Although these are natural stone slabs, you can buy paving slabs in a range of sizes to create a similar effect.

Tap the slab level, using a mallet or the handle of a club hammer, adding or removing sand if necessary. Test it by treading on the corners to ensure there is no significant movement.

Making a plinth

Make the most of a small ornament by raising it on a plinth. This will give it the stature to become a strong focal point. Sundials and birdbaths also need a plinth. You can buy these, but it's much more satisfying to build your own. Making a plinth is an easy project to start with if you've never laid bricks or blocks before — and it can be a good way to use up those left-over bricks or blocks from another project!

The picture opposite and the illustration below will give an idea of what you can achieve, and how simple the construction is. But to look right, your plinth should have dimensions that suit the object it has to support, and the choice of materials should reflect the setting as well as the ornament.

Avoid a tall, narrow plinth for a small pot or miniature bust, for example; a low plinth, perhaps 18-24 in (45-60 cm) high, can be very effective for a small object. The plinth for a sundial, on the other hand, needs to be tall enough to let you read the dial from a normal standing position.

Brick is a good material to use for a plinth positioned against a brick wall, or for one set in a border among plants. Walling blocks can look more appropriate on a patio, or in a setting where other walling blocks and concrete paving slabs are used extensively.

Walling blocks also enable you to vary the dimensions more easily, while still keeping to the basic four-brick/block pattern illustrated. They come in a variety of sizes, and many are longer than bricks. If you're using bricks, you can, of course, make the plinth larger by using more bricks for each course, but try to avoid the need to cut bricks.

A firm footing

Always prepare a firm footing for your plinth, excavating an area about 6 in (15 cm) wider than the plinth on all sides; dig it out to a depth of about 6-9 in (15-23 cm). Fill this with a concrete mix, ensuring that the top is level and just below the surrounding surface so that the footing won't be visible later on.

Use bricks or walling blocks, laying them as described for earlier projects. Build your plinth to the required height, then top with a paving slab. It's as simple as that.

You can leave it as it is for a bird table, or position your ornament or sundial. Unless the ornament is very stable and not especially valuable, it's best to fix it in position with a small dab of mortar or an appropriate adhesive.

Reinforcements

You shouldn't need to reinforce a small plinth, but if it's taller than about 3 ft (90 cm), you should use a steel reinforcing rod in the centre and pour a concrete mix into the cavity. Insert the reinforcing rod into the footing before the concrete sets.

A small ornament can look insignificant unless it's raised on a plinth, which gives it a stature that makes an arresting focal point. A plinth is something you can make quickly and easily, and you don't need to buy many materials.

Useful information

You'll find all kinds of useful facts and explanations on the next four pages. They should help you to understand some of those unfamiliar terms, and get to grips with things like the best concrete or mortar mixes for particular jobs.

Aggregate
Sand or gravel (small stones) that is mixed with cement to form concrete. Sand is sometimes described as *fine aggregate*, the stones or gravel as *coarse aggregate*.

Coarse aggregate can be either gravel or crushed stone, varying in size from 0.3 in (5 mm) to 0.75 in (20 mm). If you are laying concrete less than 2 in (5 cm) thick, choose an aggregate not more than 0.4 in (10 mm) in size. See also **ballast**.

Ballast
A mix of sand and gravel, used in making concrete. The terms *all-in ballast* and *combined aggregate* are sometimes used for this. See also **aggregate**.

Bedding face
The top or bottom surfaces of a brick.

Block splitter
A hydraulic tool used to cut through bricks, pavers and paving slabs. They are usually hired.

Bond
The way bricks are staggered to spread the load along a wall, or to interlock for a path.

Bricklayer's line
A length of string (usually nylon string) stretched between pegs or blocks that acts as a guide to ensure that bricks or blocks are horizontal when each course is being laid. See also pages 8-9.

Builder's square
A wooden device (usually improvised and made at home) for ensuring that corners are at right angles. A home-made wooden builder's square is described on page 9, but you can also buy one if you prefer.

Building regulations
These apply mainly to buildings and concern such matters as the suitability of materials, prevention of damp, minimum ventilation etc. They are unlikely to apply to any of the projects described in this book unless they are actually built onto your home in some way.

Capping see **coping**.

Cavity wall
A two-skinned wall with a space in the middle, normally used in the construction of buildings to provide insulation and reduce the risk of damp inside walls. Garden walls are sometimes built with a large cavity that can be filled with soil for planting.

Cement
This is the hardening agent used for concrete and mortar. The kind usually available at large DIY stores and builders' merchants is *Portland cement* (a type, not a brand). It's usually grey in colour, though additives can be used to change the colour.

You can use additives when mixing concrete or mortar to make it more waterproof.

Masonry cement, used for mortar, already has a plasticiser added (see **plasticiser**).

Club hammer
A heavy hammer used for jobs such as hitting a cold chisel or bolster chisel (these are used for splitting bricks or blocks, for example).

Combined aggregate see **ballast**.

Coping

The top course of a brick or block wall, usually designed with an overlap to throw some of the rainwater clear of the wall. Coping is designed to prevent moisture seeping into the exposed joints on the top of the wall.

Coping slabs are usually made from concrete, but special coping bricks are available to top a brick wall.

The term is used loosely to cover both *true coping* (which has an overlap) and *capping*, which is the correct term for when the coping is flush with the wall.

Concrete mixes

Special concrete mixes are sometimes used for particular situations, but the following two formulae will cover the projects described in this book. They refer to parts by volume. It doesn't matter whether you use a bucket, a wheelbarrow or a shovel, provided you keep to the same measure for each ingredient.

1 For foundations and footings, such as the base for a masonry wall:
   • one part Portland cement
   • two-and-a-half parts sharp sand
   • three-and-a-half parts aggregate.

   Instead of separate sand and aggregate, you can use five parts of ballast.

2 As a base for paving or a patio:
   • one part Portland cement
   • two parts sharp sand
   • three parts aggregate.

   Instead of separate sand and aggregate, you can use four parts of ballast.

Course

An individual horizontal row of bricks.

Damp-proof course (DPC)

A layer impervious to water that prevents dampness rising from the ground to affect higher parts of the wall. Rolls of DPC material are readily available from large DIY stores.

A DPC is normally used only for the walls of buildings, but can sometimes be used in a garden wall.

Efflorescence

The white, powdery-looking deposit that is sometimes seen on bricks. It's caused by soluble salts migrating to the surface of the wall. You may be able to brush the deposit off when the wall is dry. Hosing or washing may only drive the salts back into the wall.

Flat-plate vibrator

A powered tool with a flat plate on the bottom, which vibrates to compact the ground or to settle sand between pavers.

Float

A float trowel has a large, flat, rectangular blade and is used to level and smooth concrete. The blade is usually wooden. The similar steel tool is sometimes called a *plasterer's trowel*, but it can also be used for smoothing concrete or rendering mortared walls.

Footing

A concrete foundation or platform to provide a stable base for a wall.

Frog

A depression on one of the bedding faces of a brick. The frog is usually laid facing upwards, except in the top course. The depression helps to bind the courses together, as mortar partly fills the frog when the bricks are laid.

Hardcore

Broken bricks or stones, used to provide a sub-base for concrete footings or foundations.

Hawk

A board used for carrying a small amount of plaster or mortar while applying it. Usually about 2–3 ft (60–90 cm) square, with a handle beneath, it provides a convenient way to carry mortar or plaster to the working position.

Header face

The short end of a brick.

Line blocks

Blocks that are placed at the corners of walls, attached to a line, and used in bricklaying to ensure that each course is laid level.

Mallet

Carpenters use a wooden mallet to drive wood chisels. Mallets with rubber/plastic heads can be used for tapping paving, bricks or blocks to level them.

Mixing mortar

The following formulae are recommended for mortar. As with the concrete mixtures on the previous page, they are given in parts per volume.

1 For bedding paving slabs or bricks, use a mortar of one part Portland cement to three parts soft sand.

2 For laying bricks and blocks for walls, use one part Portland cement to six parts soft sand, with a plasticiser added.

It's often more convenient to use masonry cement, which already contains a plasticiser: one part masonry cement to five parts soft sand.

If a stronger mortar is required, such as for a very exposed position, reduce the sand to four parts and three parts respectively.

Masonry saw

A special saw, resembling an ordinary hand-held wood saw in appearance, with tungsten-carbide teeth that are able to cut bricks and concrete blocks.

Pavers

Small brick-like clay or concrete blocks, used for paving.

Piers

Columns used to buttress and strengthen a wall. They are also useful at the end of a wall for hanging a gate.

Planning permission

You may need planning permission from your local authority for a garden wall more than 6 ft 6 in (2 m) high, or more than 3 ft 3 in (1 m) high if it's a boundary wall adjoining a highway. Consult your local authority for advice.

Plasticiser

This is usually used instead of the traditional lime to make a mortar mix that's easier to work with. The mortar is more aerated, reducing the risk of cracking if it's laid in cold weather. Masonry cement already has a plasticiser added.

Plumb-line

A weighted device attached to a cord, used to determine a true vertical. Gravity ensures that the cord hangs exactly vertical.

Pointing

The neat finishing of a mortar joint between bricks, blocks or paving slabs. See page 34 for some of the ways in which you can point brick-work. A *pointing trowel* is a small diamond-shaped trowel with a pointed end.

Render

A thin layer of mortar applied to an exterior wall.

Sand

Everyone knows what sand is, but several types are used in garden construction. *Sharp sand* (sometimes called *concreting sand*), which is

coarse and gritty, should be used for concrete. *Soft sand* (sometimes called *builders' sand*), which is finer, is used for mortar.

Straight-edge
A long, perfectly straight piece of wood, used to support a spirit-level that by itself is not long enough to span the area being checked.

Stretcher face
The long side of a brick.

Tamp
To bang down and consolidate (hardcore or sand, for example).

Tie see **wall tie**.

Trowel
There are various kinds of trowel used by builders. The three most common ones are a *bricklayer's trowel,* used for handling and placing mortar (the blade has a flat surface, tapering to a point); a *pointing trowel,* which is similar but smaller; and a *float trowel,* which is used for smoothing concrete or a mortar render (see **float**).

Wall tie
A wire or wire-mesh device, mortared between bricks or walling blocks at points of potential weakness, and to 'tie' together two separate twin walls either side of a cavity. Wall ties are available from large DIY stores and builders' merchants.

Weep hole
A small gap left at intervals at the base of a raised bed or retaining wall, to allow moisture to seep away. See pages 50 and 52.

Index